ALL DAY LONG, THESE BABY ROBINS GOBBLE UP GRUBS, BEETLES,

AND WORMS AS FAST AS THEIR PARENTS CAN BRING THEM.

Marguerite Henry
BIRDS AT HOME

ILLUSTRATED BY JACOB BATES ABBOTT

Sponsored by
THE NATIONAL WILDLIFE FEDERATION
Washington, D.C.

AN M. A. DONOHUE BOOK

Hubbard Press
Northbrook, Illinois

To Ralph B. Henry
who hatched and brooded this book

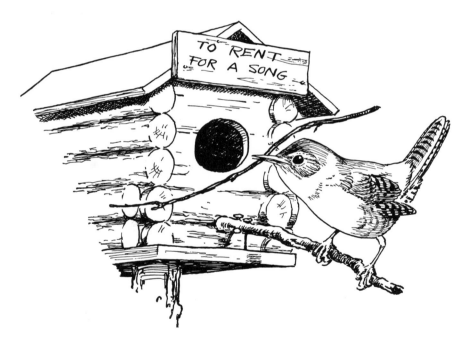

Library of Congress Catalog Number 72-81208
Standard Book Number 0-8331-0305-9

Copyright © MCMXLII by M. A. Donohue & Company
Copyright © 1972, Hubbard Press, a division of
Hubbard Scientific Company, Northbrook, Illinois 60062

Printed in the United States of America

INTRODUCTION

Marguerite Henry

To keep body and chirp together

From being a boxed-in city mouse as a child, I found it enchanting as a grownup to be turned loose in a new world of animals, birds, and green growing things. Freedom began when my husband and I rented a little Hansel-and-Gretel cottage that was scooped out of a ravine. It was like living on an island in a sea of trees. Our only neighbors were families of birds, and I wanted desperately to meet them on their own terms.

Having been born and raised in the city, I could barely tell a blue jay from a bluebird, or a thrasher from a thrush. But I had heard that if you want to know a subject, the quickest way to learn is to write a book about it.

So I set out boldly and brashly to write a bird book. Not only did I intend to know my neighbors' names, but I also wanted to find their nesting houses, see the color of their eggs, and learn whether they were seed-eaters, weed-eaters or meat-eaters. What would be the fun of having such charming friends for neighbors if I couldn't invite them to our picnic table and serve their favorite foods?

While still waiting for our furniture to arrive, I presented my very green self to Rudyerd Boulton, ornithologist at the Field Museum of Natural History in Chicago. I explained that I was about to write a book about the common everyday birds people might see in their own backyards.

Patiently Mr. Boulton tried to discourage me. "It would take a lifetime of study and observation," he said.

Impatiently I listened. Then in a voice timid yet resolute, I said: "It would be nice if you gave me a list of birds to look for. You see, I plan to do the book, and I promise not to bother you again until it is finished."

With his list in my hand, I went home in ecstasy. The book was on its way! And, as it happened, so was our furniture. The crates were scarcely unpacked and the place tidied up before I promptly began to untidy it. Upstairs and down, the little cottage became a workshop for the making of bird foods.

Washtubs in the basement were just the right size for incubating mealworms. A mealworm, I had learned, was as succulently delicious to a bluebird as a sirloin steak is to man, the only difference being that the bird gobbles dozens of mealworms just for an appetizer! This, of course, meant that the laundry tubs could never be used for their intended purpose. Instead they were filled with soft layers of sawdust and wetted down to encourage the breeding of worms.

And our kitchen! That room was in a constant bustle of preparation, as if Christmas were just around the corner. We rolled peanut butter into little balls and studded them with sunflower seeds. Chunks of suet, begged from the butcher, had to be cut into smaller chunks and stuffed into loosely knit bags so that the woodpeckers—hairy and downy—could probe inside for niblets of goodness. Walnuts had to be cracked for the chickadees and nuthatches. They, willy-nilly, had to share them with another neighbor, a gluttonous red squirrel, which we named Henry VIII.

By the time the first snowstorm swooped down into our ravine, our refrigerator had become a storehouse of bird food. Two shelves were jammed with jars of doughnut crumbs, bags of suet, leftover bacon bits and cheese rinds. Atop the refrigerator, sacks of sunflower seeds and millet stood like soldiers in a row. We wanted to be sure that as winter deepened and sealed the land, our feathered neighbors would have no trouble keeping body and chirp together.

Sunup to sundown it took me two years of watching, feeding and listening to meet 21 families of birds and to write the book.

The nicest ending was that Rudyerd Boulton, after he read the manuscript, not only suggested the title *Birds at Home,* but offered to write the foreword!

FOREWORD

In *Birds at Home,* a lively and accurate book on the family life of common birds, the author has happily chosen to present factual information in a joyous way.

Facts are interesting to children and to adults alike, and when they are expressed in good, everyday English they become positively exciting.

Here there is neither the technical and unfamiliar verbiage of the scientist nor florid romanticism.

Parents would be well advised to read this book to avoid the embarrassment of being corrected by the younger set.

Rudyerd Boulton
Research Associate
Field Museum of Natural History

CONTENTS

COLORED ILLUSTRATIONS

WITH A BEAKFUL OF WRIGGLING INSECTS FATHER WREN SINGS AT HIS GOURD NEST.

CHAPTER ONE
Birds to the Rescue

BIRDS are nearly always hungry—especially baby birds. Their appetites are as big as their mouths, and their parents never have to coax them to eat. Some nestlings eat as much as they weigh each day. That is why birds are important to farmers and gardeners, and to everyone who likes berry patches, green gardens, and fields of golden grain.

Birds save millions of dollars worth of crops every year by devouring such pests as bugs, grubs, mice, and weed seeds.

A tiny Humming Bird, no longer than a child's finger, thinks nothing of eating a hundred insects at one meal. To a Flicker, five thousand ants are just a tasty snack. Thirty grasshoppers do not begin to satisfy a Catbird; he is ready for a second helping in no time. Scarlet Tanagers can eat thirty-five gypsy moths a minute. Two thousand mosquitoes are just a fair day's catch for a Purple Martin. And a frisky little Chickadee enjoys about five thousand moth eggs between sunrise and the time he goes to sleep.

If human babies ate as much in proportion as some baby birds, they would weigh about fifty pounds when they were only a week old.

As nearly as men can figure, there are almost six billion birds in the United States—more birds than people! For every family of four people there are about two hundred birds.

If two parent birds and four baby birds can destroy fifty thousand insects in one season, think what six billion birds can do! How would our gardens grow without help from the birds?

Different families of birds eat different kinds of pests. Sparrows, for example, hunt on the ground. They destroy tons upon tons of weed seeds. Other birds, such as Robins, Starlings, Thrashers, and Wood Thrushes like to dig their food from under the ground.

Woodpeckers are grub-eaters. They spear their meals out of tree-trunks. Wrens and Chickadees like to trap the tiny insects that hide in the bark. Baltimore Orioles and Scarlet Tanagers hunt for hairy caterpillars among the leaves of the trees.

Like policemen of the air, Purple Martins sweep into space and catch gnats, mosquitoes, and flies on the wing. Owls and Hawks eat mice which cause no end of damage to grain fields.

But the most exciting fact about birds is the way they hurry to the scene when swarms of grasshoppers or other insects attack a rich orchard or a new green field. Even though some of them are seed-eaters, and others prefer grubs, they all seem to forget about their favorite food. Like firemen called to a big fire, Bluebirds, Starlings, Goldfinches, Orioles, Robins, Grackles, and Sparrows fly to the rescue from all over the countryside.

Some birds even bring their youngsters along. They line them up on a fence and treat them to an endless meal of hoppers. In a few days the insects are gobbled up. Then the plump birds fly back home, and the field or orchard begins to grow green again.

No wonder more and more people are giving food, water, and nesting houses to the birds! Men are just beginning to learn how important birds are to them.

WHEN SWARMS OF INSECTS ATTACK A GREEN FIELD, THE BIRDS FLY TO
THE FEAST AS IF MOTHER NATURE HAD RUNG A GIANT DINNER BELL.

CHAPTER TWO

The Sparrow

THE English Sparrow is a little bird with a big history. About a hundred years ago, a man named Nicholas Pike brought eight pairs of Sparrows to this country from England. Soon other men followed his example. They expected this lively little brown bird to eat up the green canker-worms that were attacking our shade trees. Then they hoped he would clean up other bugs and grubs until some day there would be no insect-pests in the United States.

The Sparrows did feast on the canker-worms, and they made themselves right at home. They built their nests almost anywhere. Today there are flocks of English Sparrows in every village and city in the United States. They stay with us summer and winter, chirping even on blustery days when there seems to be nothing cheerful to chirp about.

Some people call the English Sparrow a rowdy. They say that he moves into houses built for Bluebirds and Purple Martins; that he nips young buds and vegetable sprouts, and samples ripe red fruit. But even with these bad habits, there are plenty of good things to be said about him. He gobbles up great numbers of maggots which would otherwise turn into house flies. He destroys the vicious army worm. He eats ragweed seeds that cause hay fever. And when great black clouds of insects settle on garden crops or grain fields, he and his relatives join the rescue squad in great numbers.

English Sparrows are good to their children. They line their nests with layer upon layer of feathers. Then when March winds blow, the babies snuggle down in their feather beds and just let the winds howl.

Usually the nest is tucked in some cozy corner of a building or in a hole of some tree. But when these birds build a nest on a branch, it is shaped like an Eskimo house, with a small entrance near the bottom. The father bird helps with the building, and when the mother bird goes off hunting, he will even sit on the eggs. You can tell him from his little wife by the black chin feathers which look like a ferocious beard.

There are forty kinds of Sparrows in the United States, but the English Sparrow and the Song Sparrow are the ones we are most likely to see in our back yards. Although they look alike, the two birds are really very different. The Song Sparrow is a native of the United States. He is not a beautiful bird, but he is a musician, one of the finest in all his family. His notes ring high and clear, like the tinkle of a music box. He sings in flight. He sings in the rain. He sings at night. Even when he has hungry babies to feed, he has time for a snatch of song. And instead of repeating the same old tune over and over again, he has at least half a dozen songs all his own.

The songs of many birds are a warning to keep feathered neighbors away from their nesting territory, but Song Sparrows seem to sing just for the joy of singing.

The best way to tell the Song Sparrow from the English Sparrow is by the brownish stripes on his breast that come together in a dark blotch. And when he flies, his tail flips up and down like a teeter-totter. It looks almost as if he gets more power out of his tail than his wings.

People who are proud of their lawns are especially fond of this little striped songster for he eats enormous quantities of dandelion, crab grass, pigeon grass, and other weed seeds. One bird can eat thirty-eight weed seeds a minute! Then when he has youngsters in the nest, his beak seems to be dripping with insect-pests all the while he is not singing. He usually gathers more insects than his small beak will hold, and they stick out like whiskers.

Song Sparrows weave nests of grass and hide them under weed stalks or in shrubs. Cats often pass right by the brooding mother or the babies without seeing them because they are the color of brown earth and dry grass.

The name Sparrow comes from an old English word meaning *Flutterer*. If you have ever watched the birds flapping and fluttering in their dust baths, you will agree that the name fits them as neatly as their feathers.

CHAPTER THREE
The Starling

STARLINGS are city birds. Whistles blowing, bells ringing, lights blazing—nothing seems to bother them. They build their nests on sky scrapers, in church steeples, hollow trees, or nest boxes—anywhere there is room enough for a bundle of sticks, straws, and feathers.

Then they add their own whistles and squeaks to all the other city sounds. From high up on a dead limb, they put on long recitals, playing nearly all the sound effects in the bird band. They drum like a Woodpecker, whistle like an Oriole, and miaow like a Catbird. Not all of their music is noisy. Sweet trills, warbles, and chirpings are all part of the program. Actually, they can sing the songs of so many birds that no one is quite sure whether they are clever mimics or master singers.

In the midst of the sweetest chirping, they suddenly begin to wheeze and creak like a screen door in need of oiling. This must be their theme song, for it begins and ends nearly every program.

Starlings are like some people you know. They never look quite the same. In spring their bills are yellow as dandelions, and their black feathers shine with green and purple lights. In autumn their bills turn dark, and their feathers are tipped with white, looking as if the birds were covered with little diamond-shaped snowflakes. Only their tails

remain the same. These are always square and stubby, as if the birds had never quite grown up.

Starlings do not hop like other birds. They bustle. They travel in little companies over green lawns, pecking at insects with their dagger-like beaks. They never walk in a straight line, but scurry helter-skelter, here, there, and everywhere.

There is nothing helter-skelter about their flight, however. Their sky work at sunset is most fascinating to watch. Thousands of them fly together in perfect formation. They circle, dive, and zoom like a great fleet of airplanes. Then they flutter down like leaves and settle in the tree-tops or on the roofs of buildings for the night.

The Starling, like the English Sparrow, is not a native of America. In 1890, forty pairs of the shiny black birds were brought over from England and set free in a park in New York City.

Ten years later the men who were making our laws in Washington heard unfriendly reports about this bird. He was accused of liking cherries and tiny vegetable sprouts too well. And someone had seen him shove a Flicker family out of its nest. Someone else complained that the Starlings were a noisy nuisance to the community.

No one had anything good to say about the bird. No one thought to mention his devouring the deadly Jap beetles that harm our lawns, the canker-worms that attack our trees, the rose beetles that destroy our roses, or the grasshoppers, crickets, and dozens of our other garden enemies. No one mentioned that his traveling in flocks is a good thing when swarms of insects light on a rich field, and that often the Starlings are the first army of birds to fly to the rescue.

And of course no one said that any bird able to whistle and sing on

a frosty winter morning cannot be *all* bad.

With only the unpleasant reports on their desks, the men in Washington made a law. The law said that no more foreign birds could be brought to the United States without special permission. It also said that no one could carry the birds from one state to another.

But what did the little spangled Starlings know about laws? While the men were writing out the law, the birds were actually flying across state borders. Today there are millions upon millions of them. They are found over the entire country.

The Starlings are happy here. Like the English Sparrows they have come to stay. America is rich in green lawns, with plenty of bugs and grubs. It is their promised land.

18

CHAPTER FOUR
The Robin

ROBINS believe in the coming of spring long before people do. While there are still lace edges of snow around the flower beds, Robins are singing from the tree-tops. "Cheer up! Cheer up!" they noisily shout, as if they wanted us to understand how sure they are that spring is here. To prove it, they begin building their mud nests almost at once.

In an average spring, there is more than enough mud for Robins and everybody. But in dry weather, the mother bird has to stir up her own mud. She hops into a bird bath or pool and then scratches in the garden until her toes are covered with mud.

Up in the nesting tree, she scrapes off this mud with her beak. Then the little artist molds a neat mud nest to cement the straws and rags which she and her mate have gathered. To make the inside smooth and roomy she twirls round and round, pressing outward with her plump body until the nest is shaped like a bowl. When the mud is dry, she lines it with a fine grass mattress. From below, the nest looks straggly, but inside it is a thing of beauty, especially when it holds the treasured eggs! Robins' eggs are the color of the sea. They are so beautiful that the color, *robin's-egg-blue,* is named for them.

At first, baby Robins seem to be nothing but bobbing heads on long rubbery necks. All day long they gobble up grubs, beetles, and worms as fast as their parents can bring them. They never seem satisfied.

Grown Robins have pretty husky appetites themselves. They like to eat about fourteen feet of earthworms a day. The early morning is the best time to trap these worms. The birds scamper across the lawn and suddenly stop short. Then they cock their heads, *not to hear the earthworm*, but the better to see him. If they did not turn their heads sideways, they would not be able to look over their big yellow beaks. The minute a Robin is sure he spies a worm, he darts his beak into the earth and comes up tugging one of the slippery creatures. It seems to stretch and stretch like a rubber band, but the Robin backs and pulls until he gets it all the way out, and then gobbles it greedily.

Many people believe Robins live on nothing but worms and cherries. Yet they eat some of the greatest enemies of our lawns. Wise berry growers who want to save their fruit, plant wild berry bushes around their orchards, and the Robins pick the wild fruit every time.

If anything pleases a Robin more than a wild cherry tree, it is a bird bath. He loves to soak in the tub, but if another bird so much as shows himself, he begins splashing furiously. After his bath he polishes each feather. Just when you think he is neatly dressed for the day, he often hops right back into the water, and begins all over.

Robins are among the best known birds in the land. Really they are not Robins at all but gray-backed Thrushes. They were named by the Pilgrim Fathers who, when they first saw this native Thrush with the red breast, were reminded of their loved little Robin Redbreast in England.

In winter the birds travel over the southlands in great wild flocks. They roost far away from cozy gardens or orchards, and no one ever hears them sing. But when March comes, nothing can stop them from hurrying back to their summer homes. There, in the same old apple trees, the nest-building begins, and the air becomes noisy with Robin-song.

ON WARM DAYS MOTHER ROBIN GOES OFF ON SHORT HUNTING TRIPS

WITH FATHER, BUT ON COLD DAYS SHE SELDOM LEAVES THE NEST.

CHAPTER FIVE
The House Wren

THE busiest little birds in the bird kingdom are the House Wrens. From the minute they arrive in spring, there is not a moment to spare. Mr. Wren flies north ahead of Mrs. Wren. He has to locate the right neighborhood for a nest. It must be lively with spiders and insects.

As soon as he finds a happy hunting ground, he sings like mad from every pillar, post, and tree. This is a musical warning to all the feathered world. It means: "NO TRESPASSING. KEEP OUT!" But the warning is music as light and airy as flecks of sunshine. How much nicer than putting up a black and white sign!

To keep other male Wrens away, Father Wren begins to build nests in every possible nesting place. Wren houses are fine, but there are seldom enough to suit the busy builder. He has been known to tuck twigs in everything, from trousers on the line to mail boxes, sprinkling cans, old hats, Oriole's hammocks, even toy sand pails. From dawn to dusk he is busy carrying twigs, many of them longer than he is.

Surely when Jenny Wren arrives, she should be pleased with one of the nests he has begun. So he sings and sings until his bubbling notes guide her to his whereabouts.

What a sprightly pair they make! The pattern of their feathers is exactly alike, neat dark bands on wing and tail feathers, and the faintest of bands on their breasts. But there the resemblance ends. Jenny is a scold. She can not sing. She just sputters about everything. Not a single

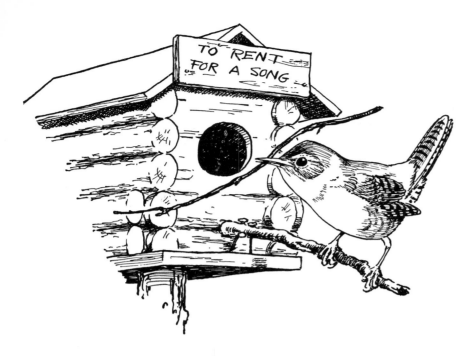

nest pleases her. "Tsk, tsk! What rubbish!" she seems to say, her little tail keeping time with her chatter, and her head wagging.

Then she chooses a nest, tosses out all of her mate's twigs, and builds to suit herself. She fills the hole so full of twigs, wire, nails, and hairpins that there is barely room for her and her little freckled eggs. Sometimes there are over seven hundred twigs in one nest. Luckily she covers the sharp twigs and nails with a cushion of feathers so they will not prick the baby birds.

Jenny is a bustling housekeeper. Each season she raises two broods and for both of them she must have clean new nests. The youngsters are well-fed, too. The parents think nothing of serving them a thousand meals a day. What is more, they have music with their meals! The father bird sings even with a beakful of wriggling insects.

No birds are more valuable to the orchard and garden than a family of Wrens. Like little brown dwarfs, they peer into every bush and bark crevice for white grubs, Mayflies, caterpillars, and spiders.

When the leaves begin to turn brown in autumn, the Wrens' feathers grow in darker, too, and they take to the woods for a little while before flying south. There they match the fall colors so well that only people whose eyes are as sharp as Wrens' can see them.

Wrens do not grow to be as old as larger birds. No wonder then they are so busy! They have to crowd a lifetime into two or three short years.

24

CHAPTER SIX
The Cardinal

No OTHER red bird has a high crest like the Cardinal's. It looks like a tall crown, and gives him a kingly air. When he mounts to the top of a tree and whistles his three cheers, he commands attention from the entire neighborhood.

He is a proud bird, and handsome too. Except for a beard of black, his plumage is bright red from crest to tail, even his beak is red. That good-sized, powerful beak adds splendor to his appearance. And it is a handy tool when he is cracking hard-shelled seeds for his young ones.

Lady Cardinals are smaller than their mates and brownish in color, but they are remarkable birds because they can sing. Most lady birds can not sing a note. They just twitter and cheep and scold. But lady Cardinals' voices are soft and lively as spring itself. They echo their mate's "Cheer, Cheer, Cheer-r-r-r-r."

The Cardinal is one of the most popular birds in the land. No less than four states—Illinois, Indiana, Kentucky, and Ohio—have chosen him as their state bird. It took more than handsome red feathers to win such honor. As the people of these states say, "The Cardinal is the crested prince of the bushes: a good father, a polite neighbor, and above all, a very great gentleman."

A Cardinal's idea of a cozy nesting spot is a tangle of vines over-growing a porch, or a shelter of evergreen trees. Both parents help build the nest, and the singing goes on at a merry pace all the while. Strips of bark and weed stems are twined into an airy nest and lined with soft moss and rootlets.

To feed two, or sometimes three broods, Cardinals need a fair-sized garden for themselves. So they keep a sharp eye on strangers. Even their own reflection in a window will set them worrying and scolding. They will often move on to a new location just because "that handsome fellow in the window" refused to come out and settle the property-question like a man. It is a good idea to cover the window with a piece of cloth if you wish to keep the Redbirds in your garden.

Once the property problem is settled, family matters go along more smoothly. The mother bird lays three or four lavender-speckled eggs and takes her place on the nest. Meanwhile her mate brings her the things she likes best to eat: fat worms and green grasshoppers.

Like a soldier he stands guard, and at the first sign of cats or hawks, he sounds his alarm: "Chip! Chip!" As soon as the enemy has fled, he throws his head back and whistles in high spirits, "Cheer, Cheer! Cheer-r-r-r!"

When the eggs are hatched, the father has little time for song. He must scurry around from sunup to sundown, catching insects and cracking seeds. Before long he has to take complete charge of the babies, for the mother bird is busy building a new nest for the second brood.

By autumn, all the youngsters have lost their dull baby feathers. They look exactly like their parents—red helmet, shiny black beard and all.

Instead of flying south for the winter, the whole family stays at home. What do they eat when the snow flies? There are all sorts of weed seeds and winter berries. And often thoughtful people spread feasts of sunflower seeds and nut meats. Just the flash of their red feathers against the snow is worth the price of many dinners.

26

CARDINALS LIKE TO WINTER IN THE VERY SAME GARDEN WHERE THEY SPENT THE SUMMER, ESPECIALLY IF THEIR HUMAN FRIENDS SET UP A LUNCH COUNTER SPREAD WITH SUNFLOWER SEEDS AND NUT MEATS.

CHAPTER SEVEN
The Mourning Dove

MOURNING DOVES are found in every state in the land. Where there are trees, they nest in them. Where there are bushes, they nest in those. Where there are neither trees nor bushes, they nest on the ground, on window ledges, hay stacks, or almost anywhere.

But oh, what nests! A skimpy handful of sticks and straws loosely twined in a careless cradle! You can poke your finger through in a dozen places. The parents themselves are not too satisfied with their nest. Even after the mother bird is brooding two snow-white eggs, the male bird keeps bringing her more twigs. She tucks them underneath her, with no thought of arrangement.

Of course the nest is not safe. Neither is it warm. But the parents make up for their flimsy building. They almost never leave their shivering twin babies alone. The mother bird covers them at night and the father bird by day. Soon they grow so big that when a parent sits crosswise over them, two little heads and two little tails peek out on either side.

The parents are great actors. If a stranger comes too near, they flap noisily to the ground as if their wings were broken. Then they whirl and flounce and make such a hubbub that the enemy chases them and forgets about the babies. And that is just what the clever birds intended, for

29

as soon as the enemy is at a safe distance, they rise in the air and fly away.

Mourning Doves belong to the pigeon family. Like true pigeons, they raise their nestlings on "pigeon's milk." This looks something like sour cream, and forms in the crops of both parents.

Instead of opening their beaks wide like other birds, baby doves put their beaks in the parents' mouths and drink the pigeon's milk.

For a week, the twins' beaks are enormous. Then, gradually, they shrink and grow horny. When this happens, the parents know their children are growing up. So they hurry off to a weedy garden or grain field and gather tiny seeds by the thousand. These are softened in the pigeon's milk until they make a wholesome cereal for the babies.

Grown doves are so fond of weed seeds they can eat nine thousand at one meal. Ragweed seeds are their special favorites. People with hay fever know all about ragweed. When they come near it, they almost sneeze their heads off. They should feel like saying "Thank you, friend!" every time they see a Mourning Dove.

Of course doves like grains, too, but they eat waste kernels. At harvest time you can see them strutting in and out among the stubble, enjoying their own harvest feast. Afterward they hunt up some fine gravel, as chickens do, to aid digestion.

If windstorms do not blow too many nests away, a pair of doves may raise five sets of twins a season. So a family of doves in every garden could do as much good as a boy digging weeds from daylight to dark.

By autumn when the families join in flocks, it is hard to tell the older children from the parents. They are all plump-chested gray birds with small heads and long tails. They have a black mark on both cheeks and a faint patch of rainbow feathers on their necks, but the gayest thing about them is their bright pink toes. Every one of the flock walks with toes turned in, so when people do that, we call them pigeon-toed.

Some flocks winter in the southern states and some migrate as far as Mexico and Central America, but they never stay away long. One windy March morning you will hear a mournful, far-away call: "Ah-Wooo-Wooo-Wooo-Wooo!" It is repeated over and over, like a mysterious echo.

Many people think it is the saddest bird song in the world, and that is why the birds are called Mourning Doves.

Really they are not sad at all. Between songs they soar high into the sky. With wings outspread they sail in wide circles, then dive swiftly to earth. Up again they zoom, until their wings whistle with the wind.

Soon they begin hunting for twigs and straws, and a soft cooing is heard as the birds pick up their nesting materials to build in the same old neighborhood. "Ah-Wooo-Wooo-Wooo-Wooo" is their song of contentment and hope.

CHAPTER EIGHT

The Baltimore Oriole

IT IS winter. The old elm tree is bare. But away up high on the tip of a bough hangs a gray cradle. When the wind blows, it rocks and trembles. But it does not come tumbling down. It was hung there by the master nest-builder of the bird world, Lady Baltimore Oriole herself.

With her sharp little bill, she wound ten, twenty, thirty, forty loops of string and plant fibres around the forked twigs. Then, clinging to the framework like an acrobat, she wove the fibres in and out, this way and that. She added horsehairs to make it strong, and bits of cotton and wool to make it soft. And she knit the sides loosely so that every spring breeze would puff through the cradle and fan her babies.

What a safe little pocket it is! Cats would not think of crawling out on the spindly twig where it hangs. And crows and hawks cannot even see into the dark nest.

Early in May is the time to scatter bits of string and white knitting yarn on bushes and fences for Lady Baltimore. As she wings over your garden, she may carry them off by the mouthful and start hanging her cradle in one of your shade trees.

Lord Baltimore does not help with the nest building. In a tree-top near-by, he tidies his flame-colored feathers and whistles. He does not try to mimic other birds. He has a whistle all his own and warbles just for the

32 🪶

AFTER THEY LEAVE THE NEST, THE PLUMP LITTLE ORIOLES FOLLOW
LORD BALTIMORE AROUND, SQUEALING "TEE-TEE-TEE! TEE-TEE-TEE!"
THEY ARE ALWAYS BEGGING FOR A LITTLE SNACK TO EAT. IT LOOKS
LIKE A GAME OF FOLLOW THE LEADER.

fun of it. In spring his music is strong and glad. In summer he sings little scraps of song, like feathers tossed in a breeze.

Lady Baltimore enjoys weaving to his quick and lively tune. It makes her want to work faster and faster, surer and surer.

When the cradle is finished, it is so deep that the mother bird is completely hidden when she sits on the eggs. She might get very lonesome with nothing but her weaving to admire, or a patch of blue sky. But Lord Baltimore chatters to her from near-by trees.

Sometimes it is like responsive reading in church. He speaks. Then she answers. His notes sound like "Over here, dear."

And she seems to respond with, "I'm all right. Go right on with your caterpillar hunt."

Just because Lord Baltimore does not help with the weaving, he is not a thoughtless bird. A male Oriole was once seen perched over the nest through the hottest hours of the day. He was actually making a little shadow for Lady Baltimore who was sitting on the eggs.

Orioles' eggs look as if a small child had scribbled on them with a leaky pen. They are covered with scrawls and blots.

Baby Orioles are known as the noisiest cry babies in the bird world. They squeal "Tee-tee-tee! Tee-tee-tee!" all day long. Even a lovely swinging hammock does not hush them. Their parents do their best to quiet them with a nice assortment of bark lice, plant lice, click beetles, and canker-worms. These insects are greedy enemies of our shade trees and orchards.

As for hairy caterpillars which feed on elm trees, Oriole families eat pounds of them! They help to save the very trees they love best. And cotton growers say that Orioles are their best friends when tiny beetles called boll-weevils attack their fields.

Who would think that Baltimore Orioles are members of the Blackbird family? They have brilliant colors. They do not croak like the Blackbird, they sing. They do not walk, they hop.

The name Oriole comes from the Latin word *aureolus* meaning golden. Baltimore was added because the bird's orange and black feathers matched the family colors of Lord Baltimore, an English colonist.

Golden Robin, Fire-bird, Hang-nest are some of the Oriole's other names. But poets call him "a scrap of sunlight with a song."

The only time he does not sing is late August. Then he and his family hide away in the woods while they shed their feathers and grow new ones. Unlike that of most birds, their new plumage comes in just like the old. Lord Baltimore is brilliant in shining black and bright orange, with pure white wing tips. Lady Baltimore and the youngsters are quietly dressed in pale yellows and mottled browns. They are now ready to migrate.

Spic and span for their trip, they return to the garden for a few farewell songs. Then they are off for the warm countries. They wing their way over Mexico, Central America, and the Panama Canal. Finally they reach South America. There, in the green forests, their bright colors flash like jewels.

Meanwhile, here in North America, they have left a gray souvenir. It swings and reminds us that when winter is through playing tricks, the Orioles will be back. They will be back to hang another cradle in the very same elm, and to whistle "Rock-a-bye Baby in the Tree Tops" to another brood of yellow-feathered nestlings.

CHAPTER NINE
The Wood Thrush

LIKE the soloist in church, the Wood Thrush stands very still when he sings. Only his throat feathers tremble. Yet the deep bell tones that come from his almost-closed beak make people feel as if they are listening to organ music.

His evening song seems to be timed with the setting sun. He starts softly with three notes that sound like "Holy, Holy, Holy." Then he gains in power. And just as the last glow of red fades from the sky, he trills off into silence like a faint far-away bell. Then night settles down in earnest.

Wood Thrushes are as calm and peaceful as their name. The mother bird will even let gentle people touch her while she sits on the nest. But if she suspects mischief, she cries "Quit! Quit!" in no uncertain terms. This call rouses her husband who comes flying to her side. He sizes up the situation and usually settles the matter with a "Tut, tut."

He seems to trust people. He will perch right on the rim of the nest and sing his golden notes. And he does not mind an audience in the front row if only they will be quiet as mice.

If Wood Thrushes were fuss budgets like the Wrens, more people would know about them. But they prefer to live quiet, simple lives. To be sure, they run along the ground like Robins and dig up worms, but they do not gobble them greedily. They fly off to a comfortable perch and eat slowly and tidily.

Hidden among the branches, the Wood Thrush is almost invisible, especially if his back is turned. His head is reddish brown, fading into dull brown on his back and olive brown on his tail. But his plump white breast has a gay pattern of black spots, shaped like tiny spear heads. The entire family is dressed alike.

Close-up you can see the white rim around their eyes, and the tiny lines that stray off into their cheeks, like the laughter lines that some grown-ups have.

Many people call Wood Thrushes "Wood Robins." Even though they are smaller than Robins, they do have a strong family resemblance. Their bulky nests are much the same, too. However, Wood Thrushes prefer to use damp, moldy leaves, instead of mud, to plaster the twigs and paper scraps together. The finished cradle is lodged snugly in the fork of a young tree. As a rule, it is placed so low that tall people can stand on tiptoe and peek at the three or four bluish-green eggs. These look much like Robin's eggs.

The parent birds are just as apt to choose a city garden as the woods in which to raise their families. All they ask is a few trees. It seems strange that they should nest in young trees which do not provide much shade. But Mother Wood Thrush solves the problem in her own quiet way. On hot days she perches on the rim of the nest, opens her wings like a pretty brown parasol, and so keeps the babies cool.

No matter how busy the Wood Thrush may be, he never forgets his evening song. In the pauses of his melody, he hums soft notes, as if he were playing his own accompaniment. With such dreamy music to put them to sleep, no wonder the children are not cry babies. In fact, they are very superior nestlings. Instead of squealing for their meals and fluttering their wings, they wait patiently.

Sometimes the youngsters are ready to leave the nest before they are ten days old. They are quite business-like about it. They begin by exercising just one wing. The next day they flap both wings. And the following day they are pretty sure to make their first flight.

With the Wood Thrush's gift of song, it seems almost unnecessary that he should do more for the world. But he eats harmful cutworms that slice off tomato and cabbage plants at the roots. He catches moths, spiders, beetles, and grasshoppers. His long slender bill makes a neat pick to gather garden enemies that live on the ground.

In fall the birds leave for Mexico and Central America. There is no noisy roundup when they leave, no circling of wild flocks overhead, no endless twittering or harsh calls. Perhaps they do not like to say good-bye—for they disappear silently, like the sun slipping into the pocket of the horizon.

CHAPTER TEN
The Flicker

WITH a broad black streak on each side of his beak, the male Flicker appears to be wearing fierce black whiskers. The female Flicker has none.

In most bird families the children look like their mother. But Flicker fledglings are exact copies of their father. Even little female Flickers have black cheek patches until they grow up.

It seems especially nice that the children take after their father, for of all the garden birds, he is most faithful. He covers them at night with comforting wings. He hums them a cradle song until he himself drops off to sleep. He helps feed them. As for care in digging a cozy nest, he works an entire month. Of course his mate helps. They can be heard tapping away at a tree-trunk long after other birds have gone to sleep.

Although Flickers belong to the Woodpecker family, their bills are pointed instead of having a broad cutting edge like those of their relatives. No wonder they prefer to dig in a rotting tree!

Modern Flickers appreciate a ready-made house if it looks like tree bark on the outside and if the inside is deep and dark. Of course it must be lined with sawdust and chips like a Flicker-built nest.

If a Flicker discovers such a nest, his noisy, laughing "Zuc, Zuc, Zuc" rouses the neighborhood. He hammers on rain spouts, tin roofs—anything that will make a loud clatter. He shouts "Flicka, Flicka, Flicka!" faster and faster, louder and louder until the entire Flicker community knows that he is about to set up housekeeping.

When the Flicker's mate arrives, he nods and bows, and spreads his wings like a gorgeous cape with a bright yellow lining.

In a week or two, one of the pair will be seen flying to the nest with insects. It may be either the father bird or the mother. The one brooding the eggs is always fed by the other. They seem like very polite birds. If the sitter gets tired of being cooped up, he calls "Flick, Flick!", and his mate hurries to relieve him.

Enemies steer away from Flicker nests once the babies are hatched, for they buzz like angry hornets, whether they are hungry or not.

Young Flickers have tremendous appetites. They eat their own weight in ants each day. And how they thrive! In two weeks they are able to climb up the steep walls of their nests and look out over the neighborhood. They are funny little creatures, with a black bib of feathers under their chins and a polka dot pattern on their breasts.

With a buzzing brood of six to eight youngsters to feed, the parents are forever hunting ant hills. They delight in stirring up a colony of bustling ants with their beaks. Then they stick out their tongues a good two inches and poke them down all the little ant corridors. Often they lick up ants and eggs by the thousand. Flicker tongues are sticky as glue and have little prickers on the end which are guaranteed ant traps.

Ants crawl into kitchens, get into the cake box and other foods. They also spoil lawns. Without the Flickers to stop them they might spread dangerously.

For the first few weeks, young Flickers sleep under their father's wings. But soon they learn to cling to the walls of their nest like grown-ups. Their claws are sharp as a kitten's and their tails end in tiny spikes. These help the birds to cling to the wood and hang in perfect safety. Of course Papa Flicker hangs himself up right beside them.

One fine day the parents cry "Yee-up!" from below the nest. A flock of curious heads pops up out of the doorway. They have the excited look of swimmers making their first dive. Finally the bravest of the brood takes off in flappy flight. And one by one the others follow.

The family stays together until fall, hunting ants and eating huckleberries. Every day is a family picnic.

A few Flickers winter in the north, but most of them migrate to the warmer states. When they take off, the white patch above their tails flickers like a beacon. Bird men can not agree about that patch. Some say its purpose is to fool the Flickers' enemies. An enemy will follow the white patch as the bird bounds through the air. Suddenly the Flicker lights on a tree-trunk and the white spot is hidden by brown wings. The enemy must be completely bewildered, wondering where in the world that rascal with the white spot has disappeared.

Other bird men say the white patch is a signal-flag to keep the flock together. Perhaps it is like following another car on a strange road at night. The tail light ahead shows the turns in the road.

When Flicker families take off in fall, the strong-of-wing fly on ahead. Their white flags seem to say: "This is the way. Follow me."

WHEN THE FLICKER'S MATE ARRIVES, HE NODS AND BOWS, AND SPREADS
HIS WINGS LIKE A GORGEOUS CAPE WITH A BRIGHT YELLOW LINING.

CHAPTER ELEVEN
The Purple Martin

BLACK people, white people, red people—all like the Martins. Long before Columbus discovered America, the Martins were natives in this unknown land. They then lived in old Woodpecker holes and in caves.

A few of the early Indians wanted the Martins to nest near their wigwams. So they hollowed out gourds for nest-boxes and hung them on little trees. Soon whole colonies of Martins nested near the Red Men.

Their new homes were much more sociable than Woodpecker holes, and they were cozy too.

The Martins had their own way of thanking the Indians. Whenever hawks dropped out of the sky to steal the Indians' chickens, the Martins flew at them fiercely and drove them off. No wonder the little fighters were later named from a Latin word *martius,* meaning warlike!

Today, while people build miniature apartment houses for the Martins, they also copy the old, old Indian custom of hollowing out gourds for them. All races seem anxious to invite these little black members of the swallow family to live near them.

45

Besides protecting chickens, they fly through the air, snapping up mosquitoes, flies, leaf hoppers, gnats, and wasps. Many people who have Martin colonies say they never have to spray their fruit trees against insects. The Martins devour them instead.

The beak of the Martin is a regular fly trap. It is short and very wide at the base, which gives it plenty of space to bag insects.

Martins feed and even bathe on the wing. They seldom come down to earth except in springtime. Then they search along the ground for nesting materials. They choose each straw and feather very carefully, stopping every now and then for a little Swallow-talk.

In flight, the male birds appear black as coal. Close-up, they are a deep shiny blue, not purple as their name would lead you to believe. The lady birds are not shiny like their mates, and are whitish underneath, with smoke-colored chin feathers.

46

Some birds insist on a whole garden to themselves, but Martins like company. The more relatives the merrier! Sometimes there will be twenty families under one roof. Each family has its own room, of course, but often they meet on the balcony to twitter. Their voices are soft and chuckling, as if they were saying pleasant things and then laughing over their own little jokes.

When there are nestlings in each room of a big Martin house, there is great excitement in the garden. Parent birds come flying from every direction, their cheeks bulging with insects.

Martin youngsters stay in their nests until they are about a month old. When they do leave, they glide into space with the greatest of ease. It seems as if they had always known how to fly. Of course there is a weakling in the brood sometimes, and then the mother bird has to shove him into the air. If the nest is near a river and the baby falls toward the water, the mother sometimes swoops under him, her wings outspread like a fireman's net. She flutters under the baby bird and flies him to safety. Again and again she pushes him into space until he learns to use his wings. Whenever Mama Martins give flying lessons, it is a signal that the colony is ready to leave.

August is round-up time for the Martins. They flock to a near by grove before heading south. Each day new thousands join up until there is a great tourist camp of restless birds.

One morning the air hums with the beat of bird-wings. They are off! Six thousand miles to Brazil! Yet as long as they live, they come back each spring to the same old nest in North America. It may be a little one-family gourd or a grand five-story apartment house. It makes no difference. To a Martin, *there is no place like home.*

47

CHAPTER TWELVE
The Blue Jay

THE Blue Jay is a jack-of-all-trades. He can hunt insects on the ground like the Sparrows. He can hammer away like the Woodpeckers. He can hide nuts as cleverly as a squirrel. And he is as full of mischief as a puppy. His favorite prank is to tease a sleepy owl. He seems to know that the owl can not see very well by day. So he pecks at him and yells something that sounds like "Thief! Thief!", until the poor bird can not get a wink of sleep.

He is a mimic too. He can imitate the alarm notes of other birds and the wild cry of the hawk. These calls frighten little songbirds and they scatter like leaves. If they happen to be eating a hairy caterpillar or a fat beetle at the time, Mr. Jay does not object to finishing their meal. Then he flies to the tree-tops and yodels like a Swiss mountaineer: "Lee-oh-la! Lee-oh-la!" He holds his head high for the high notes, and bows low for the low notes until he looks like a jack-in-the-box.

Jays belong to the same family as Crows. They have harsh voices like the Crows, and some of their bad habits, too. Yet they are birds of great courage. They will stand up even against an eagle.

And squirrels, which most birds fear, are Mr. Jay's special delight. He likes to hear them chuck and scold when he gets into their pantries and begins eating their stock of nuts. Then he will leave the feast screaming "Thief! Thief!" No one can get very cross at him when he admits it himself.

48

COULD THAT BUTTERFLY BE GOOD TO EAT? THESE YOUNG BLUEJAYS

CANNOT GET TOO EXCITED ABOUT IT. THEY KNOW THAT ONE

OF THEIR PARENTS WILL BE ALONG ANY MINUTE WITH A TASTY

CATERPILLAR OR BEETLE. THE HUNGER CRY OF YOUNG JAYS

SOUNDS LIKE "MA-MA!"

With all these noisy habits, Mr. Blue Jay can be as quiet as a mouse, especially when he feeds Mrs. Jay as she broods the eggs. There is not a sound out of him then. He hops up from limb to limb until he reaches their nest tucked away in an evergreen tree. Then he offers his mate a tasty snack of food, and is off again as quietly as a snowflake.

Blue Jays' nests are very strong. Instead of using dry, easily-broken twigs, they snap growing twigs right off trees.

When the babies are hatched, Mr. Jay is very good to them. He feeds them until they grow fat as puff balls. This is the time of year when a few Jays have been caught stealing other birds' eggs. However, men who study birds' eating habits say that only one Jay out of nearly a hundred is an egg-breaker.

Besides, they do so many really helpful, important things that perhaps we should excuse a few mistakes. They have been known to plant whole groves of oak trees by hiding acorns. They devour an enormous quantity of little pests that are harmful to crops. Many people feel too that just because they stay with us in winter when we need the color of their blue wings, we should forgive them.

Few birds are as dashing as the Blue Jay. His wings are the blue of clear skies, and his crest is high and proud. In flight, his tail and wings open out like three graceful fans with black stripes and white edgings. A black band of feathers circles his crest and continues around under his chin like a black velvet chin strap.

A Jay's face is especially interesting. It looks as if he is wearing horn-rimmed spectacles, and he winks and blinks at you with a very wise air.

The more you watch the Blue Jay, the more you see that he does not mean to be bad. He is just an imp of mischief who enjoys a bit of fun.

51

CHAPTER THIRTEEN
The Grackle

OF ALL the birds that bustle about our lawns, the Grackle acts as if he were most important. For one thing he is bigger than either Robins or Starlings. And his tail, instead of being flat like the other birds, is shaped exactly like a shoe horn. He swishes it from side to side when he struts, as if he owned the whole garden.

In the shade, Grackles look like ordinary black crows. In the sun they become dazzling creatures. Their heads are a shiny blue-green, and their tails and wings show a deep purple tint.

There are three races of Grackles in the United States and they are as much alike as triplets. The main difference is that the Purple and Florida Grackles have purplish backs, while those of their middle west cousins are bronze. All three races have the shoe-horn tails and staring yellow eyes like glassy buttons.

There are all sorts of stories about the Grackle. Some say he is nothing but a corn thief. It is true that he likes to tear the husks open and nibble the milky kernels. To make matters worse, he never finishes one ear, but enjoys snatching little samples here and there.

As a matter of fact, he saves far more corn than he ever eats. In spring he follows the farmer's plow and pounces on harmful grubs as fast as the plow turns them up.

Then when he has a nestful of four or five baby birds to feed, he brings them beak-loads of insects from daylight to dark. Wise farmers should feel like saying, "Blackbirds, all is forgiven! By all means help yourself to a few kernels of corn."

Grackle youngsters lead very sheltered lives. Their cradle is fastened high in an evergreen tree. It is made of mud and grasses, much like a Robin's nest.

About the only thing Grackle parents do not do for their young is sing to them. However, they go through all the motions of grand singers. They spread their wings a little, fan out their tails, lean forward with feathers a-quiver and beaks wide open. Then all that comes out is a rusty squeaking known as the wheelbarrow chorus.

Even young Grackles have hoarse voices. You can sometimes hear them squawk greedily when their parents find a piece of bread on the lawn. If the bread is quite stale, the parents soak it daintily in the bird bath before offering it to the impatient children. Grackles also enjoy wading in our bird baths or along the shores of rivers or lakes. They have a funny habit of holding their tails high so as not to get them wet.

Toward autumn Grackle families join up in great black gangs. Each night they can be seen flying low over house-tops and trees on their way to a good roosting camp. Their shoe-horn tails make good rudders to steer the way. At times there are so many birds it looks as if a streamer of black ribbon was flung clear across the sky.

By November the roosts are deserted and the wheelbarrow chorus is whanging away in the Southlands.

CHAPTER FOURTEEN
The Ruby-throated Humming Bird

THE Humming Bird is the feathered acrobat of the air. He can dart straight up like a sky rocket. He can fly sideways. He can do dives, and loops, and spins, and turns. He is the only bird in all the world that can fly backward. But most amazing of all, he can mark time in the air. Of course his sturdy wings hold him up. They beat so fast they look like twin shadows. With a slow motion camera it is possible to count fifty-five wing beats a second.

As if these stunts were not enough, the Humming Bird has another trick. He can swing swiftly back and forth in a wide curve, as if hanging from an invisible point in the air. All the while his wings hum in their rapid beat. To the pioneers of America, who had never seen such a tiny bird, this humming sounded like a "Humble-bee." So they called him the Humbird.

Without stopping, the little Hummer can fly straight across the blue waters of the Gulf of Mexico, a distance of five hundred miles. With a good tail wind, he can do a mile a minute easily. Then his wings beat eighty times a second.

He is a cyclone in feathers and the tiniest bird in the whole world— so tiny that he actually bathes in beads of dew. And he weighs no more than a rounded tablespoon of sugar.

Over six hundred kinds of Humming Birds live in America, chiefly in Central and South America. Of all the family, only the midget Ruby-

A HUMMING BIRD'S NEST IS ABOUT THE SIZE OF A SILVER DOLLAR. HARDLY ANYONE WOULD EVER FIND IT—EXCEPT FOR THE ANXIOUS PARENTS. THEY DART TOWARD IT, SQUEAKING IN THEIR CRICKET VOICES AND BUZZING NOISILY WITH THEIR WINGS.

throat nests in eastern North America. Even he likes to spend his winters in the flower-tangled jungles of Panama.

But the moment pink and white blossoms cover our fruit trees, he reappears as if by magic. His greenish feathers shimmer like silk, and the ruby at his throat, which is called a *gorget,* blazes in the sun.

In a few days the Lady Hummers arrive. They are not shiny bright like the males, and they have no ruby gorgets. But they are artists. They can fashion a tiny cup of a nest that looks as if it had been spun by fairies. Silky plant fibres and the fluff of dandelion seeds are laced down with cobwebs. Patches of moss form the delicate walls.

Only spiders and Humming Birds can work with gauzy cobwebs. Mother Hummer wraps them around her bill and unwraps them at the nest. Then she shapes the soft materials until she has formed a perfect little cup. By the time the cradle is fastened to the side of a bough with the glue from the spider's web, people and birds often look right at it without seeing it. They mistake it for a moss-covered knot. It takes a week to finish this elfin nest.

Two little eggs, no bigger than kernels of puffed rice, are laid in the cup. They are guarded well. If another bird casts a shadow anywhere near the precious eggs, Ruby-throats declare war. No matter if the bird is an eagle or a hawk! Quick as an arrow the midgets dive and dart at the enemy with their sword-like bills. Their voices become harsh, rasping sounds, and the air is alive with the hum of their wings. They seem everywhere at once. No wonder the big birds are soon glad to let these flying swordsmen alone!

Baby Humming Birds are hatched without any fuzz or feathers. They look more like sleepy beetles than Humming Birds. It is good that their nest is woolly and soft, for even when the feathers begin to grow, they are nothing but sharp spines. Often the nestlings live in their cradle from three to six weeks. It gets such hard wear that the mother bird has to keep patching the walls to keep the babies from falling out.

After the twins leave the nest, the Mother Hummer sometimes meets one of them on the wing and feeds it while they both seem to be "standing still" in the air. They look like puppets on invisible threads.

Although the babies are born and raised in quiet woods, they are soon eager for the bright flowers of cities and villages. Wherever there is a yard with red, orange, or pink flowers, they stop for lunch. Dipping their long beaks in the petal cups, they sip the sweet nectar, along with any chance insects. If there are not enough insects in the flowers, they snap them out of the air.

A Humming Bird's tongue is a remarkable tool. It looks like two tiny drinking straws joined together. Then at the tip it opens out into a kind of spoon-shaped brush. The birds can thrust their tongues out like daggers, spoon a drink of honey, clean up tiny spiders, and be off to the next flower before you can say "Ruby-throated Humming Bird!"

Hummers consider sugar-water a luscious substitute for flower honey. It is fun to watch them drink out of a tiny bottle tucked in an artificial red flower. Lawn sprinklers are another invitation to these midgets. They fly through the spray like tiny rainbows, and they do not mind being watched at all. In fact, these gleaming mites seem to fear nothing. In a storm, when most birds fly to cover, they spread their wings as if to catch every rain drop.

No one has ever seen a Humming Bird walk or hop on the ground. They are airy creatures of the sun, the wind, and rain.

CHAPTER FIFTEEN
The Brown Thrasher

THE Brown Thrasher is the brown bird with the big tail, the big beak, and the big voice. He is nearly a foot long, but almost half of him is tail. When he hunts among the leaves, his tail seems to work as hard as his beak. It thrashes back and forth, making little rustling noises against the dry leaves. Whoever named the bird Brown Thrasher, made it easy for everyone to recognize him.

The Pilgrims, however, called him their Planting Bird. While they were sowing corn, this strange bird would mount to the top of a tree and sing for an hour at a time. His voice rang out above all other bird songs. It was not just an ordinary song; it was a talking song. He seemed to be saying actual words. To the Pilgrims it sounded like:

"Hurry up, hurry up; plough it, plough it;

Harrow it, harrow it; drop it, drop it;

Cover it up, cover it up; I'll pull it up, pull it up."

Sure enough, he did pull up a few young sprouts. Bird men say

59

he was looking for cutworms that attack new corn. The Pilgrims did not know this, but they liked the lively bird anyway. They could put words to his song and sing them in their minds as they worked.

Today, the Brown Thrasher still sings his planting song, even though he may be far from corn fields. He sometimes builds his big bulky nest in city shrubs—if the owners have not raked their lawns too neatly. Nothing makes a finer hunting ground for bugs and grubs than last year's leaves.

When it comes to locations, he is a fussy bird. He insists upon having tangles and brambles. The more tangled the vine or the more thorny the tree, the better he likes it. Hawthorn trees are especially safe. The sharp thorns are like sword's points guarding the nest. Any busybody who runs into the thorns is sure to leave in a hurry.

But few enemies wriggle their way into the little jungles where wise Thrashers nest. If a nosey cat comes too close, the parents dart at him with their beaks and slap at him with their wings and tail. Then they hiss the snooper away. Often their calls are so loud that all the birds in the neighborhood fly to the rescue.

Thrasher parents divide the homework. They take turns sitting on the four or five brown-flecked eggs; and they both feed the young. How they ever find their way back to the nest is Thrasher magic! It looks exactly like the criss-crossed twigs that support it.

The birds make quite a ceremony of their return trips. With a couple of fat beetles in their beaks, they half-run, half-fly across the ground. As they approach the nesting thicket, they glance around quickly to see if they are being watched. Then up they hop, twig by twig, like repair men climbing a telephone pole.

If you are close enough you can hear the excited cries of the baby birds. Then there is deep silence while they devour their dinners. Four baby Thrashers can eat over fifteen hundred insects an hour. Luckily, this is in spring, the very time of year when insects do most damage to young crops.

Some people mistake the Thrasher for the Wood Thrush. But one glance at that long wagging tail spells T-h-r-a-s-h-e-r. Besides, the Thrasher has strange yellow eyes, as if the sun were shining inside them. And his breast is striped instead of spotted. Then there is his song. He sings in the sun and hides when it is gloomy. The Wood Thrush does just the opposite.

When Thrashers go south for the winter, they stop in comfortable thickets along the way. Each thicket seems cozier than the last, so it takes them a long time to reach the Gulf or South Atlantic states.

A few never do get there. They stay on and on, like people enjoying a party. There are plenty of acorns to eat and winter berries to pick. And almost before they know it, white hawthorn petals take the place of whirling snowflakes, and May beetles stir under old leaves. Then, from the topmost bough, "Hurry up, hurry up; plough it, plough it" rings out above the lively sounds of spring.

CHAPTER SIXTEEN
The Bluebird

ONCE a Bluebird found a vacant nest box on a tall pole in the center of a garden. He tried the doorway for size, and explored the inside. It suited him so well that he flew straight up in the air for joy, singing his three glad notes as he flew.

Then he staked off about a hundred yards of property. Instead of driving little pieces of wood in the ground, as men do, he warbled his ownership in outbursts of song.

A lady Bluebird happened to be winging north at the time. She heard the light notes and came over to investigate. She was a tree-trunk bird. That is, her parents and grandparents had always nested in the cozy hollows of dead trees.

But this nest interested her. Cats could not climb the slippery pole. Nor could they hide in shrubs or trees close by, because there were none. And Starlings could not squeeze in the entrance because it was too small.

For nearly a week there was much serious twittering. Then one day the male bird's three notes had a glad ring. And the lady bird's two notes sounded just as happy. Apparently they had agreed on the weather-beaten nest-box.

Almost at once they began carrying wisps of grass in their beaks. They placed them

well in the back of the box for safety. Although the nest was nothing more than a lining of soft grasses, it took a week to build. There were so many things to stop and twitter about.

Besides, the pair had to take their daily baths and preen their feathers. This was quite a performance. Unlike other birds, they ducked their heads under the water while they sloshed their tail and wing feathers. Then they opened their wings to the sun and fanned themselves dry.

Occasionally both birds had to stop and defend their nest. Sometimes a busy Wren would poke her twigs right in the doorway, or another Bluebird threaten to set up housekeeping on their property. Then their danger-call rang over the garden. It was a single low note, almost as gentle as their song. But there was nothing gentle about their fighting!

In spite of all these interruptions, Mother Bluebird found time to lay four little eggs that matched her pale blue feathers. Both birds took turns sitting on the eggs, though Mother Bluebird usually took the longer shifts. She would look out of her little port-hole and watch for her mate to bring the refreshments. Fat worms and caterpillars pleased her especially.

Except for a few silky whiskers, the baby Bluebirds were quite black and naked when they hatched. But their appearance improved at a great pace. In two weeks they were fluffy and speckled, with a definite hint of blue in their wing and tail feathers. With all their speckles, it was easy to see that they belonged to the Thrush family. Their little black beaks proved it too. Like the Robins and all the other Thrushes, they had a tiny notch in the upper bill.

As soon as the downy babies could fly, Father Bluebird taught them the many uses of their beaks. He showed them how to peck worms, beetles, crickets, and spiders off the ground; and how to find caterpillars on the trees. He also introduced them to the delights of eating wild grapes and blueberries. It was fun to be grownup!

While the youngsters were out hunting with Father, Mother Bluebird was repairing the nest for the second brood.

It is well that Bluebirds raise two or three broods a season, because the number of Bluebirds in the world has been growing smaller. Ice storms, cats, and other enemies have killed off far too many.

Bird men say that there is a serious shortage of Bluebird houses. People seem to be chopping down all the dead trees. As a result, the snug nesting holes are cut down too. In some places, Bluebirds have actually been forced to build their nests in rural mail boxes!

To make up for the house shortage, people are now building thousands of Bluebird nest boxes each year. They are rent-free to the bird "with the sky on his back and the red earth on his breast."

No birds are finer guests than the Bluebirds. They help to clean up garden pests. Their voices are never harsh. And their blue feathers are like flowers in the garden. They seem to enjoy every minute of their stay, for they are among the first birds to arrive and the last to leave.

Of course they will never be window-sill birds like the Sparrows or Chickadees. They are half-wild, half-tame creatures, the blue forget-me-nots of the air.

MOST BIRD YOUNGSTERS ARE OFF TO EXPLORE THE WORLD AS SOON AS THEIR WINGS ARE STRONG. BUT BLUEBIRD BABIES OFTEN COME BACK TO VISIT THEIR MOTHER WHILE SHE IS HATCHING A SECOND BROOD. THEY HAVE EVEN BEEN KNOWN TO HELP FEED THEIR NEW BROTHERS AND SISTERS.

CHAPTER SEVENTEEN
The Catbird

HE MAY be just a little slate-colored bird, but the Catbird is an imp in feathers. He hops along the picket fence or skips from bush to bush, keeping pace with anyone in the garden. He is as curious as a cat. Picnics under the apple tree, clothes flopping on a line, children playing—everything seems to interest and puzzle him.

But if he is puzzled by us, we are amazed by him. At one time he is gay as a feather. His tail stands up like a flag pole. His beady eyes dance. His dusky coat is shining and beautiful. The next time you see him, his feathers droop and he looks like a rag bag.

His tail seems to be a weather vane, showing how he feels. If it tilts up like a Wren's, he feels fine. If it wags madly, like a Brown Thrasher's, he is angry. If it jerks merrily, he is feeling very chipper. If it droops, he feels droopy.

Strange to say, the Catbird's notes are as changeable as his spirits. One minute his voice is soft and low, the next it is harsh and tuneless. "Miaow!" he yowls; or whines "Mew, Mew," like a hungry kitten.

In Spring when he returns from the south, he sings with a southern accent. He is a clever mimic in bird calls and other sounds. You would think your garden was full of tropical birds. And you rush out to find just one little Catbird making all that music.

After a few days he forgets the southern

67

birds and begins to imitate his new neighbors: Robins, Song Sparrows, Orioles, and Wood Thrushes. Without stopping he runs one famous song right into the next. And just for fun he tucks in a few cat calls, the squeak of a wheelbarrow, or the glug-glug of a frog. All the while he jerks his tail back and forth to emphasize his notes.

Sometimes he mocks the frightened peep of a lost chicken. And he does it so well that the mother hen flutters and clacks as if to say, "Oh, how could one of my brood be hidden in that lilac bush!" And then soon, the little imp is mocking the squawking hen.

When the Catbird's mate comes up from the south shortly after him, he greets her with a low bow. Then you can see the lovely patch of cinnamon-colored feathers underneath his tail. Except for that small patch of color, Catbirds are dark as smoke. Even their toes and beaks are black. But it is not a dull black. It is shining like satin.

The dusky little pair like to build their nest close to people's houses, but they hide it so deep in the shrubbery that only a bird or insect can slip in without getting scratched.

The instant the male bird hears a twig crack, he snarls and hisses like a cat. Meanwhile the mother bird spreads her wings to hide the deep blue eggs. She hunches her head down into her feathers like a man huddled into a big overcoat. Often every catbird in the neighborhood joins in the angry chorus until the enemy slinks away.

The nest itself looks like a brush heap, but it is strong and roomy enough for a family of four or five. After the babies are hatched, the father bird does more mewing and less singing. Only occasionally you can hear his cradle song. It has a strange muffled sound because his beak is nearly always stuffed with insects.

Very little garden fruit is touched by Catbirds. They actually prefer tasteless mulberries or sour dogwood berries. For every home-grown cherry they pick, they are known to destroy a thousand insects. All day long, the parents are busily rushing to the nest with plump green caterpillars, potato bugs, and crickets.

Just as human babies clasp a grown-up's finger, Catbird babies are continually grasping the little root linings of their nest. In this way they develop their toe muscles so that they are able to perch on lacy twigs when they grow up.

Toward autumn, the entire family goes berry picking. The young ones look very wise as they swing on a honeysuckle twig and suddenly dart off with one of the bright red berries in their beaks. The youngsters' feathers soon look as satiny as their parents'.

There is every reason why a Catbird's feathers should shine. He dresses them most carefully. A cold shower in the morning is always followed by an hour's polishing with his bill. And before he goes to sleep for the night, he cleans each feather all over again.

He even uses his claws for a comb. Then he fluffs himself up like a feather bed and drops off to sleep. But if the moon is bright, he has time for only a catnap. Soon he wakes up and sings all the snatches of song in his memory. He weaves these scraps together like a patchwork quilt and then spreads them lightly over the stillness of the night.

CHAPTER EIGHTEEN
The Red-headed Woodpecker

WHO cares that the Red-headed Woodpecker can not sing? Least of all, Red-head himself! Let other birds do the singing. He prefers to be the drummer in the bird band. "A-rat-a-tat-tat! A-rat-a-tat-tat!" he beats the sharp tapping notes, using a hollow tree trunk for a drum, and his long beak for a drumstick.

Even with all his noisy drumming, the Red-headed Woodpecker is a prim bird. He looks like a fat man wearing a stiffly starched white shirt and a spotless black and white coat with tails. His head is covered with crimson feathers that come to a deep V on his breast. And his mighty beak is flattened at the tip so that it makes an excellent chisel for carving out nesting holes.

Mr. and Mrs. Woodpecker nearly always dig their nest in the same dead tree trunk or telephone pole they used the year before. The two birds work in shifts. Mr. Woodpecker chisels away at a merry pace. Then Mrs. Woodpecker takes a few blows. First they cut a round doorway. It is so perfectly round that a biscuit-cutter could not have done a neater job. Then they drill out the hallway and dig down, down, down until they have scooped out a cradle for the babies. Little chips of wood and plenty of sawdust form a soft warm cushion.

Woodpeckers' noses are lined with tiny hairs to keep them from breathing the sawdust as they drill, and their heads are big and heavy to give plenty of weight to their hammering.

WOODPECKERS LIKE TO "HANG THEMSELVES UP" WHEN THEY REST. THEY CLING TO THE BARK AS IF THEIR TOES WERE TINY HOOKS, AND THEIR STIFF TAIL FEATHERS ACT AS BRAKES TO KEEP THEM FROM SKIDDING DOWN THE TREE TRUNK. WHEN THIS BABY GROWS UP, HIS HEAD WILL TURN CRIMSON JUST LIKE HIS PARENTS'.

There is good reason why Woodpeckers dig their nesting holes deep. If the nest were out in the open, red-headed Mrs. Woodpecker and her five or six shiny white eggs would be very conspicuous.

Young Woodpeckers do not look like their parents. Their heads are brown instead of red; so their awkward trial flights are not very noticeable. As soon as they become good fliers, good woodcutters, and drummers, their head feathers turn a beautiful crimson. It is almost as if they were given a red badge for good work.

Most members of the Woodpecker family—like the little Downy Woodpecker and the big Hairy Woodpecker—use their chisel beaks for digging tiny tunnels beneath the bark. Then they poke their long prickly tongues down the tunnel and spear a wood-boring beetle or a grub. Redheads dig for their food sometimes, but they want variety in their meals. They like to swoop into the air and snatch insects on the wing, or dive to earth for a lively grasshopper or ant. They also like picking berries, husking corn, and gathering nuts.

When autumn comes, they care nothing for the weather. It is the supply of nuts and acorns that counts. If they are plentiful, then let the winds howl, let the snows fly! The Redheads will stay at home through the long winter. If tiny insects get into the acorns, they relish them as much as the nutty seed.

But some winters the beechnuts and acorns are scarce. Then the Redheads wing south. They do not fly in a straight line like other birds. They soar into the air and then dip low as if they were riding a roller coaster. Occasionally they will stop to play "A-rat-a-tat-tat! A-rat-a-tat-tat!" on a tin roof or a hollow tree. It is a rousing farewell from the red-headed drummer in the bird band.

CHAPTER NINETEEN
The Slate-colored Junco

NO NEED to go to the woods to find the midget Junco! Wait until some snowy, blowy day and the Juncos will come to you—whole flocks of them. And instead of hiding away up in the tree-tops where only field glasses can spy them, they come right to your door yard.

Scatter canary seeds or chicken feed on the ground; put dabs of peanut butter on the bushes . . . and listen to the Juncos twitter your praises. Those pink beaks may be tiny, but they can crush seeds in true Sparrow style. The birds roll them over and over in their beaks until the shells are soft enough to crack. Then they enjoy the goodness inside.

Juncos really are Sparrows, but only young Juncos have the tell-tale Sparrow streaks. Hardly anyone gets to see the youngsters, however. They are hatched far away in the wilds of Canada or Alaska, or in cool mountain regions of the United States.

With the first frosty days in September, little families of Juncos come down out of the north. They travel from one weed patch to another, cleaning up weed seeds. But along with the first snowflakes, little flurries of Juncos hurry around to our houses.

"Dark winter skies above and white snow below"—that is how the poets describe their colors. Their outer tail feathers are white, too, and the air is alive with white streaks as the birds bounce and dart from one bush to another.

These lively Snowbirds have their own ways of keeping warm. They sleep in dense evergreen trees or burrow their way into a haystack. Then all night long they perch first on one foot and then on the other, so that four little toes are always tucked under downy feathers. It would be hard to hop on frost-bitten toes!

Morning finds their appetites sharp as icicles, and back they hurry to our door yards. Where snow has melted, they have long cool drinks. And when the snow is dry, they take flutter baths, raising little clouds of powdery snow until the birds are screened behind a white shower curtain. After their baths, the cold wind ruffles their feathers and gives them a good dry cleaning.

In spring, before the flocks leave for their northern nesting grounds, they sing soft trills, entirely different from their low twittering. These trills are little samples of spring music for us to enjoy until Orioles, Wrens, and Thrushes arrive from the south to give us full measure of song.

Then one evening in April, the brave Snowbirds are off for adventures in the North, their tails flashing white V's against the sky. Perhaps the V stands for Victory—Victory over snow, and wind, and ice.

75

CHAPTER TWENTY
The Goldfinch

PLUMP and yellow as butter balls, the Goldfinches travel in merry companies, holding song festivals in the air. Sometimes their voices sound far away. Then suddenly they burst into noisy melody, like a chorus of canaries. That is why people call them Wild Canaries.

The remarkable thing about Goldfinches is that they can sing and fly at the same time. They rise and dip through the air as if they were skimming over little invisible mountains. At the top of each curve they sing "Per-chic-o-ree"—their notes sliding downhill just as they themselves dip down.

In late summer when many birds think about returning south, the Goldfinches are just ready to build their nests. Even then they do not grow sober with care. The male bird hovers over a tree, singing at the top of his lungs. He seems to be pointing it out as a fine place to nest.

Mrs. Goldfinch is as merry as her husband. Instead of working all day like the Flickers, she puts in a busy hour or two in the morning and again in the late afternoon. Between times she and her husband rise and dip through space like tiny yellow boats on blue waves. Life is fun for the Goldfinches. Yet they are wise parents.

No one builds a stronger nest than Mrs. Goldfinch. She weaves plant fibers together and bunts them with her breast until the tiny cradle is firm and strong. Usually it is lodged in a maple tree where the broad leaves can act as umbrellas for the babies. When the cradle

IF THE MOTHER BIRD LEAVES THE NEST FOR A MINUTE, PAPA GOLD-
FINCH CHASES HER BACK. HE IS GOOD-NATURED ABOUT IT, OF
COURSE, BUT THERE IS NO MISTAKING THE FACT THAT HE WANTS
THOSE LITTLE EGGS KEPT WARM.

is finished, Mrs. Goldfinch tucks in a mattress of thistle-down. Then she lays from three to six pale blue eggs.

People who do not know Goldfinches might easily mistake the pale yellow mother for a nestling. When she hears her mate sing as he comes to bring her food, she opens her beak and flutters with excitement. But hardly anyone mistakes the bright male. He is a handsome bird with black wings, and a crown like a shiny black pompadour.

When the nestlings are hatched, the parents do not fuss and fret over them. In a few days the mother bird accompanies her husband when he goes off to gather weed seeds. It takes each bird about half an hour to crack open the seeds from one thistle head and store them in their crops. By the time the parents return to the nest, the seeds are soft as porridge.

One day Mama Goldfinch does not deliver the food to the nest. She perches below and sings a "Come and get it" song. Timidly, one by one, the babies flop down a branch or two to be fed.

Soon the whole family has fun together—splashing in pools, drinking diamonds of dew, and swinging on flower heads.

When they gather in a dandelion patch, it looks as if a pillow fight is going on. Clouds of white fluff sail into the air as the birds unwrap the seedlings at the base of each dandelion tuft.

By fall the Goldfinches are again traveling in merry companies. They are all dull colored now, but they still swoop in joyous flight. They may drift south a short distance, but they seldom travel far. They are always ready to stop wherever there are dried sunflowers or hollyhocks. They will crack the seeds until the husks fly, warbling a few golden notes, like flashing memories of dandelions on a hillside.

79

CHAPTER TWENTY-ONE
The Black-capped Chickadee

FUTURE policemen—every one of these tousled Chickadees! In another month they will be tumbling over twigs, swinging upside down on branches, and capturing thousands of tiny insects that escape the bigger birds. Each family is a regular squad of policemen, "on duty" twelve months a year. In winter they seize sleeping insects hiding in the bark. In summer they pounce on leaf hoppers, moths, and all the troublesome pests that try to damage our shade and fruit trees.

People who love trees as well as birds often put up log houses for these feathered guardsmen. But whether the Chickadees choose a hand-made box in the garden or an old Woodpecker hole in the woods, they never fail to enlarge it. Five to ten frisky Chickadee youngsters need room to grow. After the parents have chipped out a bigger house, they carry every bit of sawdust out of sight. They seem to think it best not to let anyone know about their building operations.

Even with an over-sized house, there is no spare room. When the youngsters are hatched, they have to fit around each other like the parts of a jig saw puzzle.

Chickadees must need a great deal of warmth for they sleep on a mattress made of rabbit's fur, fine moss, and wool. Apparently they need warmth inside and out, as the parents are constantly stoking their little furnaces with good, hearty food. They serve the little ones about a meal a minute.

Often the parents do a relay race. The mother bird pops into the door with a load of moths. Just as she is popping out again, she meets her mate. He gives her the beak-load he was about to deliver, and she hustles right back in again to begin the feeding all over.

Other birds go south in winter, but the plump little Chickadees stay at home. They are not the least bit grumpy about it. Even in snowstorms they lisp, "Tsick-a-dee-dee-dee-dee" in great glee. And they come close to our windows where we can admire their shining black caps and gray and white uniforms.

After Christmas, human friends of the Chickadees often set their Christmas trees outdoors, and decorate them with delicious doughnuts, peanuts, and pine cones dipped in fat. Then *every* day is Christmas for the excited Chickadees. They hang from the branches like live ornaments, and their te-dee-ing fills the air like the tinkle of sleigh bells.

CHAPTER TWENTY-TWO
The Scarlet Tanager

FINDING a Scarlet Tanager is like winning a treasure hunt. There are all sorts of clews. The first clew is an oak grove or an old apple orchard. The second clew is his call note, a crisp "Chip chur-r-r."

Most people think his song sounds like a Robin with a sore throat. But unlike the Robin, he seems to whistle and hum at the same time, as if he were playing a duet all by himself.

Usually the Scarlet Tanager is heard long before he is seen. Then suddenly from away up high in the tree-tops, there is a flash of scarlet and black feathers. His inky black wings and tail make his scarlet body seem even brighter.

It is a double-feature surprise when anyone discovers this shy Redcoat, for his strange mate is likely to be close by. She has not a single red feather to her name. Her dress is the color of new-green leaves.

Who would ever think this odd pair could be mates? But they are, and apparently very happy. He feeds her plump caterpillars while she broods the eggs. In fact, he is one of the best caterpillar hunters of the feathered tribe. Even if a caterpillar rolls himself up in a leaf, the Scarlet Tanager knows just how to pull him out. That is why he is called the guardian of the trees.

Of course he never sits on the nest—not with his plumage the color of fire and coals! But his little mate is quite safe there, even if her speckled green eggs are not. The cradle of sticks and stalks may be airy and

FATHER TANAGER IS TEASING HIS YOUNG ONE TO FLY
BY HOLDING A TASTY MORSEL JUST OUT OF REACH.

cool for the nestlings, but a few have been known to fall through the slats! Sometimes the mother bird has to build two or three nests a season before she finally raises a successful family.

The youngsters have much downy grey fuzz about their heads when they are hatched. When they leave the nest, they are small copies of their mother, except for their striped breasts and stubby tails. The brownish stripes of the fledglings show that they are related to the Sparrow tribe. They all have the same short stout beaks, too.

The male bird is a big help with the meals. He keeps the youngsters well-fed with smooth and hairy caterpillars, potato beetles, and a nice assortment of insect pests. It seems as if he wants the entire brood to be big and strong for the flight to South America.

By the time the family is ready to leave, they are a strange looking group. Some of the little males have a touch of red in their feathers, but the father bird is now a sorry looking creature. He is changing to his dull winter plumage, and his gorgeous scarlet feathers are spattered with muddy yellow. He looks as if someone had upset a jar of mustard over him. With this coat of many colors, he and all his family wing their way to the northern part of South America.

There, in the land of the tropics, they spend the winter. No doubt they see many of the yellow, orange, green, blue, and purple Tanagers that never leave South America.

Toward spring the male bird's feathers gradually change to deep scarlet until he is again the bird of fire. When he returns to the United States, he seems to bring something of the tropics along with him—a picture memory of flame-colored flowers and deep forests. Perhaps he is the flying color-bearer from our South American neighbors.

85

CHAPTER TWENTY-THREE
The Ways of Birds

NESTS are not birds' houses. They are nurseries where the baby birds eat, sleep, and grow up. As soon as the babies are old enough to fly, they are anxious to be off with youngsters of their own age. They seldom return to their snug little cradles.

Most parents lose all interest in the nest when their children are gone. If they raise two broods a year, they immediately start building a brand new nest for the second brood. Of course there are exceptions. Some birds simply do a thorough house cleaning. Starlings, for example, often shake out the old feathers, plump them up, and repair the old nest for the new family. And a Mourning Dove has been known to use the same flimsy cradle for five broods.

But the birds that build the most beautiful cradles or the strongest ones never use them over again. Orioles hang a new hammock every spring. Humming Birds fashion a new moss cup. Woodpeckers dig a new cave. And a lady Robin would never think of using the same mud cradle, no matter how strong it was.

When the nest is finished, mother birds lay one egg a day, but do not begin sitting on them until the very last one is laid. Otherwise they would hatch on different days. As it is, all the youngsters break out of their shells on the very same day.

They chop their way out with a tiny tooth that grows on the tip of their beaks. Later they lose this baby tooth and go through life

86

without any teeth at all. This is not a serious matter. Their beaks are as good as a dozen teeth and a box of tools besides. They use them as knives, forks, and spoons, as weaving needles to build nests, as traps to catch insects, as combs to clean feathers, as crushers to grind seeds, and as daggers for fighting. Almost the minute the nestlings are hatched, those beaks open wide for food.

Human parents usually try to divide refreshments equally among their children. In bird families, the greediest bird gets the biggest helpings. The youngster that pops his head up first, squeals the loudest, and opens his mouth widest always gets the most food.

When a baby has been so greedy that he cannot possibly swallow another morsel, the parent bird removes the last tidbit from his mouth and gives it to the next noisiest bird. So the whole family makes out pretty well after all.

Birds drink very daintily, even if they do not eat that way. They take a little sip and then hold their heads high to let the water run down their throats. After each sip, they have to raise their heads. Only pigeons can keep their heads down and drink all they want without stopping.

Birds' wings have almost as many uses as their beaks. The Humming Bird hums with his wings. The Mourning Dove flaps his wings over his back to startle an enemy. Many birds use their wings to fight off cats and squirrels. But their main purpose,

of course, is to carry the birds swiftly and safely wherever they want to go.

It always seems like magic when a young bird flies for the first time. Actually, he has been practicing for days . . . fluttering and stretching to develop his flying muscles. Whenever baby birds seem restless, it is a signal they are getting ready to take off. A timid nestling can suddenly become very brave about flying if he sees his parent dangling a plump caterpillar just out of reach.

When birds go to sleep at night, they clasp their toes around a branch. No matter how soundly they sleep, those strong little toes never loosen their grip. Some birds like to sleep high in the tree-tops where every stray breeze keeps them cool. Others like to snuggle in fir trees where it is cozy and warm. But wherever and whenever they go to sleep, they sing their own bedtime songs. Blue Jays have a noisy goodnight call as you would expect. Starlings chatter. Chickadees sing a tinkly tune. Flickers hum. Wood Thrushes whisper softly. But none of the songs last very long. After all, it has been a busy day and it feels good to them to tuck their sleepy heads in their own feather pillows.